I

LISTS

Buster Books

First published in Great Britain in 2016 by Buster Books, an imprint of
Michael O'Mara Books Limited
9 Lion Yard
Tremadoc Road
London SW4 7NQ

A CIP catalogue record for this book is available from the British Library.

Papers used by Michael O'Mara Books Limited are natural, recyclable products
made from wood grown in sustainable forests. The manufacturing processes
conform to the environmental regulations of the country of origin.

ISBN: 978-1-78055-450-1 in paperback print format

1 3 5 7 9 10 8 6 4 2

Designed and typeset by Ana Bježančević
Cover and interior illustrations by Valeria Valenza
Cover design by Claire Cater

Printed in China

 www.busterbooks.co.uk  Buster Children's Books @BusterBooks

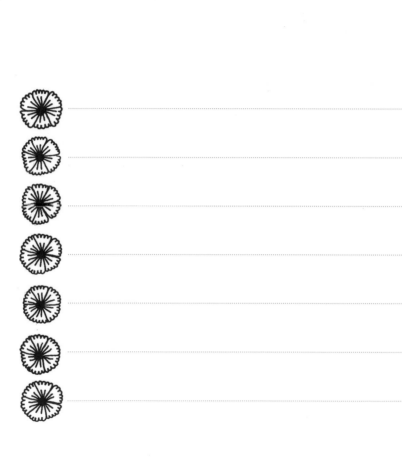

MY GREATEST EVER IDEAS

....

....

....

....

....

....

THE BEST GIFTS I'VE EVER RECEIVED

❄ ....

❄ ....

❄ ....

❄ ....

❄ ....

❄ ....

❄ ....

HIDDEN GEMS I ONLY TAKE SPECIAL PEOPLE TO

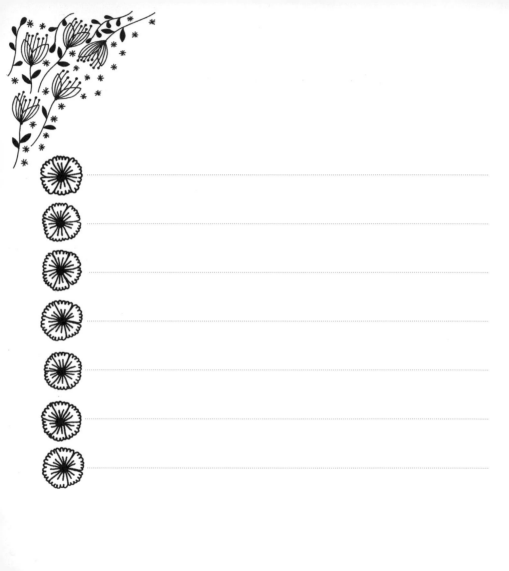

INVENTIONS I WISH WERE REAL

···

···

···

···

···

···

···

INTERESTING PEOPLE I'D INVITE TO MY BIRTHDAY PARTY

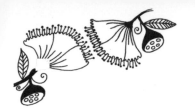

MY FAVOURITE TOYS AS A CHILD

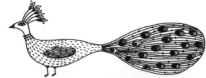

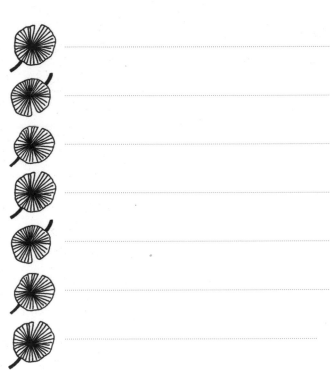

SIGHTS I'D LIKE TO SEE

FARAWAY PLACES I'D LOVE TO VISIT

....

....

....

....

....

....

TIME
MACHINE

OCCASIONS IN HISTORY I'D TRAVEL TO
IF I HAD A TIME MACHINE

PLACES I WOULD LIVE IF IT WERE SCIENTIFICALLY POSSIBLE

 ....

 ....

 ....

 ....

 ....

 ....

 ....

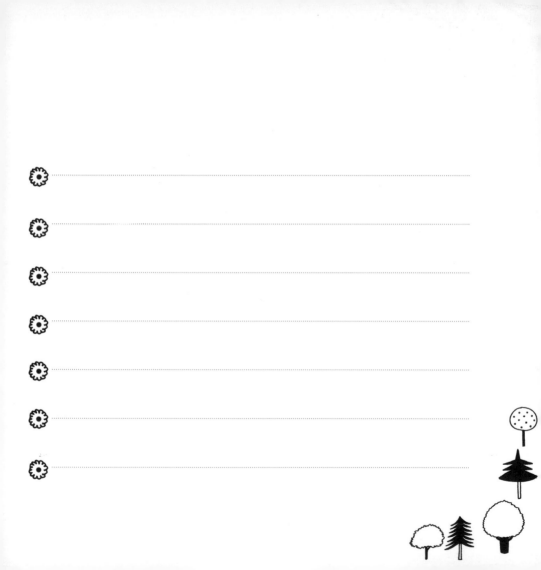

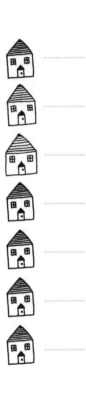

....

....

....

....

....

....

....

RIDES I'D LIKE IN MY PERSONAL THEME PARK

....

....

....

....

....

....

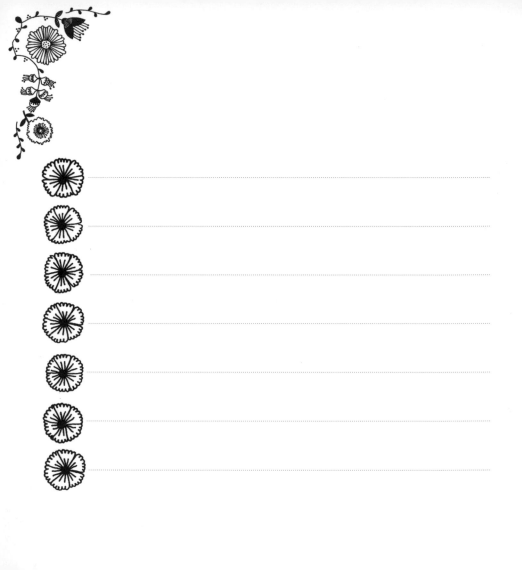

STRANGEST DREAMS I'VE HAD

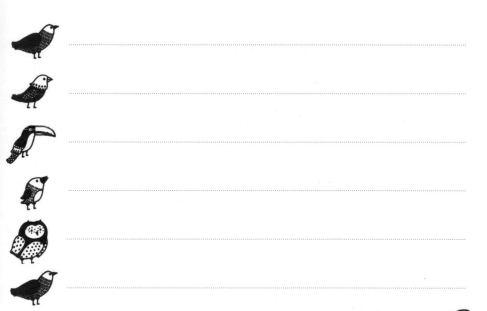

STUFF I DID AS A KID BUT AM TOO SCARED TO DO NOW

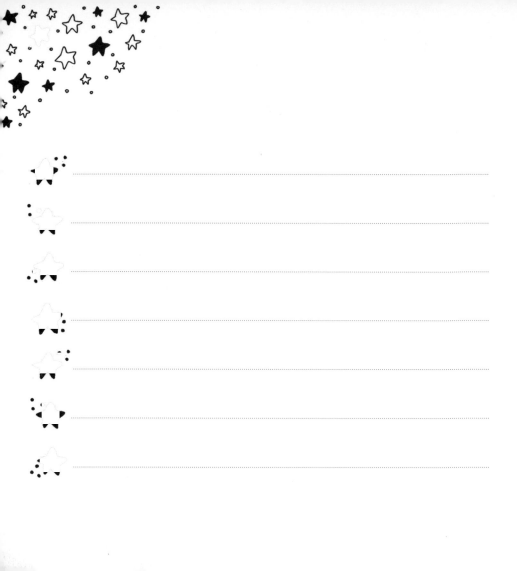

....

....

....

....

....

....

....

SUPERHERO POWERS I WISH I HAD

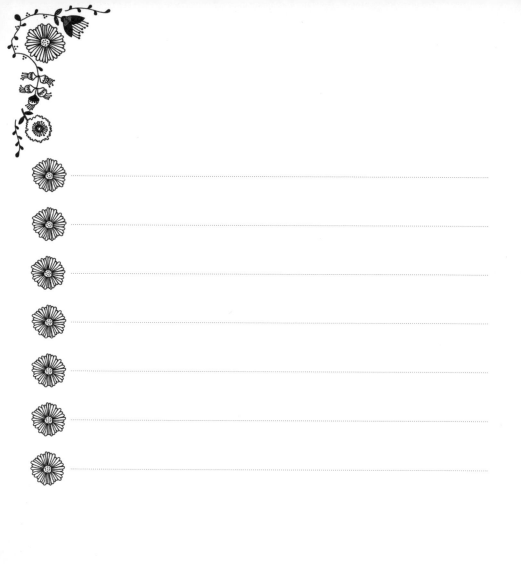

THINGS I WOULD LIKE TO DO IN SPACE

THINGS TO DO ON A LAZY SUNDAY MORNING

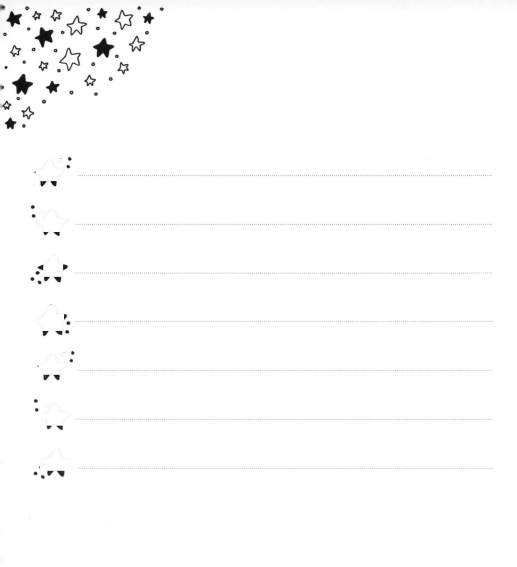

BECAUSE I AM
MAJESTIC

TOP CONTENDERS FOR BEING MY ANIMAL SPIRIT

WHAT I WOULD DO IF I WAS QUEEN FOR A DAY

WHAT I WOULD DO IF I WON A MILLION

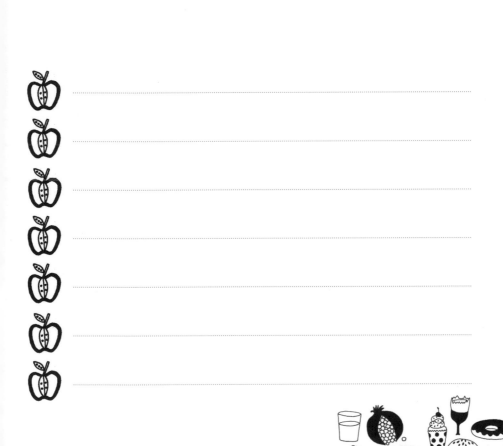

BEST IDEAS FOR FANCY DRESS COSTUMES

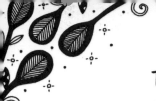

THINGS I AM TRULY PROUD OF

❋ ....

❋ ....

❋ ....

❋ ....

❋ ....

❋ ....

❋ ....